A. M. R.
BARRET

OBOE METHOD
Revised and Expanded Edition

Edited by
MARTIN SCHURING

CONTENTS

Alfred Music Publishing Co., Inc.
P.O. Box 10003
Van Nuys, CA 91410-0003
alfred.com

Copyright © MMX by Alfred Music Publishing Co., Inc.
All rights reserved. Printed in USA.

No part of this book shall be reproduced, arranged, adapted, recorded, publicly performed, stored in a retrieval system,
or transmitted by any means without written permission from the publisher. In order to comply with copyright laws, please apply for
such written permission and/or license by contacting the publisher at alfred.com/permissions.

ISBN-10: 0-7390-7744-9
ISBN-13: 978-0-7390-7744-3

Cover Painting: *The Oboe Player (or Portrait of Benjamin Sharp)*
by Thomas Eakins

A Kalmus Classic Edition

Complete Method for the Oboe

by Apollon Marie-Rose Barret

Edited by Martin Schuring

Notes to the Expanded and Revised 2nd Edition

Apollon Marie-Rose Barret (1804-1879), was the solo oboist of London's Royal Italian Opera, Covent Garden for 45 years. He was also an innovative oboe designer, devising many mechanical and acoustical improvements still in use today. To illustrate the advantages of his new oboe design, built by the firm of Triébert in Paris, he published the second edition of his *Complete Method for the Oboe* in 1862. A facsimile of that book, now published by Boosey & Hawkes, is the Barret *Oboe Method* still used today. While the facsimile provides a fascinating link with the past, its antiquated typography and many minor errors make it difficult to use, especially for younger students.

This revised and expanded second edition includes some material that was omitted from my first edition published in 2001. The reason for making some omissions is simple: not all of the book is necessary for today's oboe student. The original publication from 1862 sought to be a complete music tutor. Thus, it introduced basic music theory concepts such as the names of the lines and spaces, the rhythmic values of notes and rests, and other lessons of basic musical literacy. These have been omitted from the current publication since many excellent music theory texts now exist. This edition does include, however, several of Barret's short chapters on the subjects of playing technique, elements of style, and musical interpretation, offering a very interesting glimpse into the musical custom of the time. In the 1862 edition, these instructional texts are followed by many pages of scale exercises. These have been omitted since that material has long been supplanted by generations of fine scale books. The musical material in the current publication starts with the Thirty Scale Exercises beginning on page 46 of the 1862 edition. These were left out of my first publication, but I now believe that they are important preparation for the rest of the book and should be included. I have not included the two "Airs Varié" at the very end of the book. While they are charming and musical, the fact that they include a number of bars of rest suggests that they should be supplemented by a piano part which is now lost. In addition to these several expansions of the book, I have corrected as many small errors as I have been able to find. This book now includes everything that the modern student might wish to learn from Barret.

Dynamics and Expression

In the preface to his second edition, Barret writes, "Unless differently marked, it is a general rule that in ascending passages we should increase the tone, and decrease it in descending passages." At least half, probably more, of the dynamic markings in the book are meant to emphasize this point, or to be "differently marked." Since Barret was writing for students, he painstakingly and repetitively marks the score. But, as a warning against excessive obedience to his instruction, he immediately continues, "It is a great error to make a 'nuance' on every note. Many persons practice this exaggeration, thinking it to be expression: they deceive themselves. It is but affectation, and only shows their want of real feeling the more strongly." So, it is clear that the graphic crescendos and diminuendos are meant to be played with subtlety. Readers may refer to the following section to read Barret's complete discussion of these questions.

Many of Barret's graphic diminuendos (as distinct from the *word* "diminuendo") are not really intended to cause a reduction in tone, but rather to indicate where note groupings should begin; with access to modern music typesetting software, he might have drawn brackets in place of many of the diminuendos.

Music, like speech, has punctuation and inflection—it contains commas and periods, question marks and exclamation points, quotation marks and whispers. The difference is that music notation does not allow for these punctuations to be printed in the score; the player must find them for him or herself. Barret's use of diminuendos is often meant to show where a note grouping begins so that the student gains facility in seeing this. In the example below *(Example 1)*, the diminuendos show the beginning of each note grouping, while the carats show its conclusion. I have provided brackets to show what Barret might have notated had the typography existed.

Example 1—Showing Barret's use of diminuendos to indicate musical note groupings.

Here is another example *(Example 2)*, again showing that the diminuendos are meant to show the beginning of a musical note grouping and not a decrease in sound volume. To describe this concept in a different way, all downbeats must have upbeats, even in a tissue of uninterrupted sixteenth notes. The question for the interpreter is: how many upbeats precede the downbeat? One, two, or three? By placing the diminuendos carefully, Barret helps us to find the answer to this question.

Example 2—More note groupings shown by diminuendos

Seen this way, the apparently unmusical diminuendo in measure 1 of Melody No. 1 makes perfect sense: the G begins a note grouping which concludes on the downbeat of the second measure. Therefore, even though a diminuendo is printed, a crescendo is permissible, indeed necessary (Ex. 3).

Example 3—Suggested interpretation of Melody No. 1

When Barret writes the words *crescendo* or *diminuendo*, however, he definitely wants a corresponding increase or decrease in sound. This usage sometimes results in curiosities: see measure 39 of Grand Study No. 3, with the crescendo and diminuendos occurring at the same time.

As performing musicians, we have two duties. The first is to observe the markings on the page; the second is to make those markings sound beautiful. When we see markings that make no sense, we have to delve beyond what the composer says, and attempt to figure out what the composer might mean. These studies provide a perfect introduction to this difficulty. Until the diminuendos are seen to mean something else, the text is difficult to interpret.

Although the book is carefully (even fussily) marked, Barret also points out, "In going from a pianissimo, to a fortissimo, and vice versa, an intermediate 'nuance' is necessary to avoid an abrupt transition...." Thus, it is reasonable for the player to add some crescendos and diminuendos not printed in the score. See, for example, measures 32–34 of Grand Study No. 6. Although the word *crescendo* does not appear, it is musically and historically correct to play each measure a little louder to prepare the forte in measure 35.

Editorial considerations

The aim of this edition is to present a clean copy of Barret's original text with the errors and inconsistencies eliminated. No further editing took place. In doubtful cases (there are some deliberate inconsistencies, to be sure), Barret's original was preserved. Frequently, more than one interpretation of the text is possible, so my editorial process is explained below.

Often, the graphic marks in the facsimile are very small, or of inconsistent size, making it difficult to determine whether a mark is meant to be an accent or a diminuendo. In these doubtful cases, I have written accents when the mark indicates a meter shift (for an example, see measures 50-51 and 54-55 of Grand Study No. 16), and written diminuendos when the purpose is expressive.

Often, two or more places in the same piece appear to be parallel, but receive slightly different treatments. In these cases, I began by examining the surrounding material. Compare, for example, measures 13–16 with measures 66–69 of Melody No. 13. At first glance, only the slurring in the melody looks different, and it might be tempting to make it consistent. But there are several other differences: measures 66–69 have an added sforzando, altered articulation in the bass, and altered crescendo markings, all of which combine to allow a change in the melody's slurring as well. One misprint is likely, but three or four are not. On the other hand, there seems no good reason why measures 3–4 in melody 8 should not receive the same slurs as measures 23–24. All the other musical material is exactly the same; thus, making the slurs consistent is justified. Dozens of cases of missing staccato dots, missing dynamics, inconsistent slurs, etc. have been corrected silently without comment where appropriate.

For the most part, the arrangement of measures, lines, and pages is the same as the Boosey & Hawkes facsimile, except in cases of illegible crowding. This has added a few extra page turns to the book, but I felt the improvement in legibility was worth it.

Grace Notes

Although Barret is quite detailed in his preface about the execution of the different graces, his *Oboe Method* employs three different notations without apparent reason—it seems that the notation depends on the range of page numbers, suggesting that different technicians may have worked on the project at different times. Grace notes appear as slashed eighth notes, un-slashed eighth notes, and un-slashed sixteenth notes in different places in the book. In this edition, all single grace notes are presented as slashed eighth notes.

Performance and Practice Suggestions

Many page turns do not occur in musical places. In these instances, the student is encouraged to memorize a measure or two before or after the page turn to give a musical resolution to the phrase. Some of the etudes continue too long for performance in one breath to be feasible (Grand Study No. 15, for example). In these cases, it is permitted to stop (in a musical place!), breathe, and resume.

Students could enhance the benefit of these etudes by also transposing them up or down a semitone. This added step develops the essential discipline of playing in a key, rather than reading individual notes.

All of Barret's repeats were preserved. Many of them are important for formal reasons, but not essential in performance.

Most important, though, is not merely to learn the notes of the etudes. One of the remarkable features of this book is its rare combination of pedagogical organization and musical value. All the pieces are useful; several are truly beautiful. Appreciate the beauty, and remember that the pieces are exercises: they are meant to teach you something. Each piece is meant to teach you something slightly different. Think about it, and try to discover what it is you are meant to learn. Then, your practicing and study will be much more rewarding.

I will not be as confident as Barret when he stated, "I have carefully revised this Edition of the method and the few errors which were before uncorrected have now entirely disappeared." Any errors that still remain are entirely mine.

Martin Schuring
Tempe, AZ
March, 2010

Principles of Music

by Apollon Marie-Rose Barret

Editors note: The following are extracts from the front matter of the Barret Oboe Method. Most of Barret's idiosyncratic punctuation and capitalization have been preserved except in cases where the readability of the passage could be improved by small changes in punctuation. These short articles provide a fascinating glimpse into the musical scene and stylistic customs of the time.

THE OBOE

The Oboe, as a solo instrument, possesses the finest qualities, combining delicacy and force with sweetness and flexibility of tone, thus rendering it more capable than any other of embodying feeling with every shade and variety of expression.

In the orchestra it is indispensable, and the peculiarity of its tone, which is distinctly heard above all others, participates both of the stringed and wind instruments.

In the manufacture of this instrument, various experiments have been made to discover the wood best adapted to produce a good tone; experience has clearly proved that Boxwood and Rosewood claim the preference. I recommend Rosewood, having found that wood far superior in producing a full body of tone, which can be modified in the softest and most delicate manner: the lower notes especially are of a finer quality than in instruments manufactured of other woods.

Many endeavours also have been made to improve the tone and fingering of the Oboe. Boehm's system prevailed for some time, but the great inconvenience of that system, which diminishes the compass and changes entirely the quality of the tone, has induced me to make new researches. The Oboe, in its present improved state, is a very perfect instrument, and the modifications applied to its mechanism have preserved the fine quality of its tone in its natural state. (Barret states in a footnote that these improved oboes will bear marks from either "Triebert—Paris" or "Barret—London.")

The compass of this instrument ranges from B♭ to G alt: it has fourteen keys, two of which, having additional branches, increase the number to sixteen; from the greater length of the bell (a late improvement) the instrument derives a certainty of tone throughout, which enables the performer to produce the upper notes, such as E and F above the lines, with greater certainty. (Barret writes in a footnote that those studies including a low B-flat have been provided with alternatives for instruments not having that note.)

I would advise those persons who require an instrument to look more in point of economy to utility than to external beauty taking care it has the full complement of keys, otherwise bad habits of fingering are engendered, and which are difficult to eradicate.

In the selection or exchange of instruments, pupils should have the advice of a master, or some other competent person, as they are unable of themselves to appreciate a good instrument, or to detect an indifferent one.

THE COR ANGLAIS

The Cor Anglais, or as it may be called, the tenor Oboe, since it bears the same relation to the Oboe as the Viola does to the Violin, is capable of producing great effect, both in the Orchestra and as a solo instrument. No instrument so nearly approaches the tone of the human voice, and in Italy it is called not only the "Corno Inglese" but "Umana Voce."

The quality of its tone is peculiarly adapted to express melancholy in Music, and in Cantabile and slow movements it is unrivalled. This peculiar quality, however, unfits it for great rapidity of execution.

The fingering is precisely the same as on the Oboe, the tone produced being one fifth lower.

The Baryton or bass Oboe, is an octave lower in pitch than the Oboe, and is also fingered in the same manner; it possesses a finer quality of tone, and is heard to advantage both in the Orchestra and as an Obligato instrument.

Of these two instruments, the Cor Anglais is better adapted to the practice of amateurs, as it is not so difficult to produce a good tone on it, as on the Oboe. As the same music suits both instruments, those who play the Oboe can easily become proficient on these before mentioned varieties of it, by merely accustoming themselves to the difference of their proportions. The process of making reeds for the Cor Anglais and Baryton is exactly the same as for the Oboe, but requires the machine, tools, and cane to be of larger proportions.

In addition to these varieties of the Oboe, two others: an Oboe in B-flat, one note lower in pitch than the ordinary instrument, and one a minor third higher, in E-flat, are in common use on the Continent in military bands, and are found to be very effective, playing with the E-flat and B-flat Clarinets. (In a footnote, Barret says the following: "I shall at any time be happy to exhibit the capabilities of these instruments to Masters of Bands who may favour me with a call at my residence *31 Gloucester Street, Gloucester Gate, Regents Park*, and also to select instruments for amateurs, Pupils and others.")

ON THE POSITION OF THE INSTRUMENT

The quality of the tone depends greatly on the manner of holding the instrument; for instance, if the Oboe be held similarly to the Clarinet, it very rarely happens that a good tone is produced. The best and most natural position is to place the instrument in a straight line from the mouth at a proper declination, about six inches from the body, measuring from the thumb of the right hand. The head must be nearly erect, the arms not too far nor too close to the body, but placed naturally; the hands must rest lightly on the instrument, in a slanting position: turning them the contrary way not only has a bad appearance, but is the means of paralyzing the fingers; this must be more particularly attend to in the position of the left hand. This observation is addressed to those who play the Flute, and who are most liable to fall into this great error.

The left hand holds the top joint, and the right hand the middle joint of the instrument.

The second joint of the first finger of the left hand must not touch, nor rest, on the Oboe: it would have a similar bad effect to that which has been previously pointed out and impede the freedom of the hand.

The fingers must be placed on the instrument without stiffness, slightly curved, and raised sufficiently high, when off the holes, to allow the free passage of air; but not too much so, as that would detract from their agility.

The holes must be covered by the under or fleshy part of the first joint, not by the tip of the finger.

ON THE POSITION OF THE REED ON THE LIPS

It requires great care and practice to arrive at the best manner of placing the reed on the lips, as on *this* mainly depends good quality of tone; it is essential to adhere strictly to the following rules.

The lips must cover or close over the teeth, so as to form a sort of cushion on which the reed must rest: the blade of the reed must be placed centrally, not too far *in*, nor too far *out* of the mouth; fixed so that it does not move from its place either in producing the higher or the lower notes, which must entirely depend on the management of the pressure of the lips, and the greater or less quantity of air forced into the reed.

The best advice I can give to the Student is to practice carefully, for some hours every day, slow pieces and sustained scales: this will form the lips in the best manner and contribute greatly to improving the quality of tone.

THE TONE

However exquisite and beautiful the tone may be, it is comparatively useless if not accompanied by taste and sentiment; but it does not follow that the pupil must rely on sentiment or expression alone, and not endeavour to improve the tone; quite the contrary; his utmost attention must be devoted to that most essential point, for it frequently happens that pupils, in the earlier stages of study, have a bad tone, which may be improved by care and practice. The mode of scale study I have previously recommended will be found very useful in improving the tone.

ON THE MANNER OF "ATTACKING" THE TONE

The tongue is to Wind Instruments what the bow is to Stringed Instruments, it produces brilliant execution, and is the means of an infinite variety of articulations.

It is no easy task to make the tongue and fingers sympathize, or act together, particularly in the commencement; it is only after long practice that the pupil will succeed. The beginning of every phrase must be "attacked" with the tongue. The tonguing must be performed in the following manner.

The reed must be placed in the mouth according to the rules laid down in the article titled "On the Position of the Reed on the Lips". The tip of the tongue must touch the end of the reed, so as to close the aperture between the two pieces of cane forming the reed; the mouth is then filled with air, by the pupil drawing a long breath, retaining it, and compressing his cheeks sufficiently to cause the reed to vibrate. The tongue must leave the reed quickly to allow the breath to pass with some force into it: *this* constitutes tonguing.

The great difficulty is to sustain the note, without deviating from the quality or justness of the tone. In order to do this, the lips must be carefully kept in the position indicated at page 3 and the stream of air forced into the reed must be perfectly equal in order to finish the note, whether it be forte or piano: this requires great practice and management of the breath: care must be taken that the cheeks are not puffed out in playing.

ON RESPIRATION

The manner of breathing into the Oboe requires much management and skill. Pupils generally use more breath than is required from the smallness of the aperture in the reed. In beginning a phrase, the lungs must be sufficiently inflated for its performance. As musical phrases seldom are composed of more than two, three, or four bars, a pupil of the most delicate constitution may easily accomplish this without fatigue or exhaustion, even in a slow movement. If in playing a phrase, the pupil should find he has retained too much air, he must let a portion escape, taking care to have sufficient remaining to finish the passage. In taking breath, in the middle of a passage, it must be done quickly, by what is termed half respiration.

Breathing through the nose must be avoided. The effect of piano and forte is produced by the quantity of air and the degree of power used in forcing it into the instrument.

ON ARTICULATION

Articulation is to Music, what Accent is to Speech: it renders the playing clear and intelligible, and it is by articulation that music is made to express subject and passion, without which it can never be understood.

There are two modes of articulation: the slurred and the staccato. The first is indicated by a curved line above or under a group of notes: it signifies that all the notes so marked must be played smoothly, excepting the first, which is to be attacked by the tongue.

Example 1

The second, or the staccato, is indicated by dots, round or pointed: placed under or over each note, signifying that those notes must be accentuated, short and distinct with the tongue.

Example 2

Example 3

The difference between the two dots is, that the pointed one must be played very short, the same as it is marked in the second line of Example 2, while the rounded one *(Example 3)* must be more soft but equally distinct.

There is another mode of articulating, which unites both marks *(Example 4)*:

Example 4

This must be played each note distinct, but with a soft tongue, and the note held out to its full value.

Pupils should carefully practice these four different ways of articulating, as they contribute greatly to giving variety to the playing and form the groundwork of a good execution.

There are some ways of articulating passages more advantageous than others, particularly in solo performing; the selection must depend on which is the most effective and best adapted to the instrument. I will give a few examples

Example 5

In rapid passages of triplets requiring to be executed with vigour, No. 1 of this example *(Example 5)* is to be preferred, as suiting better the Oboe.

In passages of four notes, as in the following example *(Example 6)*, No. 1 is the most effective on the Oboe, whilst No. 3 is preferable for rapidity of execution.

Example 6

In passages of six notes as Example 7, No. 1 is to be preferred, except in a very rapid movement when it is better to take No. 3.

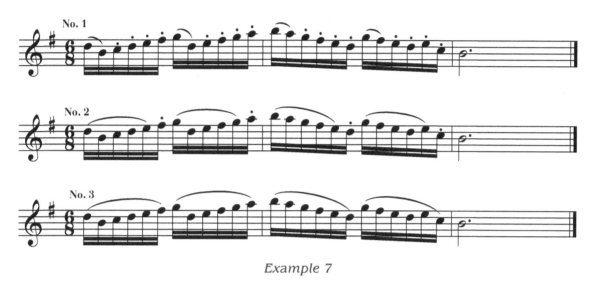

Example 7

Any of the above modes of articulation may be used; the choice must depend on the nature of the passage to which they are applied, and the time of the movement.

ON EXPRESSION

Expression, unlike those musical attributes which may be acquired by study, is only exhibited where nature has bestowed a favourable organization. Upon those who have not this gift, *no* practice, *no* study, will ever confer it. Nevertheless the habit of playing good music, and listening to the best artists, will give a notion of what is meant by it; and by taking the latter as models, one can in some measure supply the place of real expression, at all events so far as to be able to phrase correctly and without affectation.

The *"nuances"* or shades of expression, give variety to music. In going from a pianissimo to a fortissimo and vice versa, an intermediate "nuance" is necessary to avoid an abrupt transition; for instance, a phrase marked as No. 1 must be executed as No. 2 *[Example 1]*.

Example 1

Unless differently marked, it is a general rule that in ascending passages we should increase the tone, and decrease it in descending passages *[Example 2]*.

Example 2

It is a great error to make "nuance" on every note. Many persons practice this exaggeration, thinking it to be expression; they deceive themselves, it is but affectation, and only shows their want of real feeling the more strongly.

"Nuances" should be used sparingly, that is to say, it is preferable to use but one in a phrase than to destroy the good effect by frittering it away in several smaller nuances *[Example 3]*.

Example 3

In syncopated passages care must be taken to avoid marking the second half of the note *[Example 4]*. No. 1 is as it is usually marked. No. 2 must be carefully avoided.

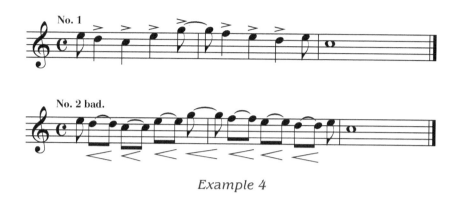

Example 4

In passages like the following *[Example 5]* it is equally necessary to avoid marking every beat in the bar, unless the composition is specially marked: No. 1 is as it should be marked; No. 2 is bad.

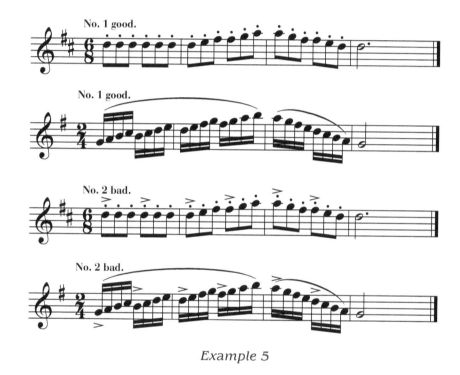

Example 5

In fact the art of nuancing which can be acquired only by a long practice of the different modifications of the tone is a great resource and I advise pupils to pay the utmost attention to this most essential part of Music.

With regard to orchestral performances I must make a few remarks. When a solo has to be performed, and the accompaniment is sufficiently subdued to allow the solo instrument scope, the soloist must use largely every means in his power to produce effect, and to predominate of the Orchestra, the solo player being, for the time of his performance, in exactly the same position as an accompanied singer. If on the contrary the Oboe be used as an accompaniment, it should be then played as piano as possible, and not be heard above the solo instrument. In soli, or passages for several instruments, the performer must endeavour to equalize and blend his tone, so as not to be heard above or below the other instruments, never making himself more than one assisting part of an harmonious whole.

ON SMALL NOTES, TRILLS, AND GROUPETTES

No fixed rules have been written on "small notes."

Their execution is entirely left to the taste and caprice of the player. This is so true, that a passage written thus *(Example 1)*:

Example 1

Can be executed as follows by one artist *(Example 2)*:

Example 2

And in this manner by another *(Example 3)*:

Example 3

And be equally good one way or the other: only Ex. 2 is more in the modern taste than Ex. 3 and of course preferable.

In our days, small notes are only employed as means of abbreviation, and in passages in which the player is in the impossibility of changing the intention of the composer, for, if there is any doubt, all the notes of the passage are written.

A point in which everybody agrees in the manner of executing small notes, is when there are several before a principal note; they must then be slurred quickly on that note in order to arrive in time on the principal note *(Example 4)*.

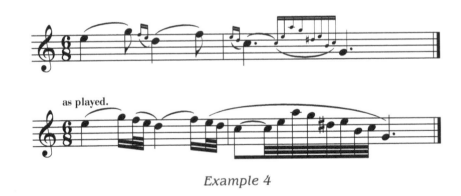

Example 4

It is the same when the distance of the small note from the principal note, is more than a tone, which can be a third, a fourth, a fifth, etc. *(Example 5)*

Example 5

The trill, or *mordente*, is a shake placed on a note of short value and which is struck as quickly as possible in order to give it more brilliancy. It is indicated as it is marked in No. 1 of the following example *(Example 6)*, but it must be executed as in No. 2 of the same example especially if it is a moderate movement.

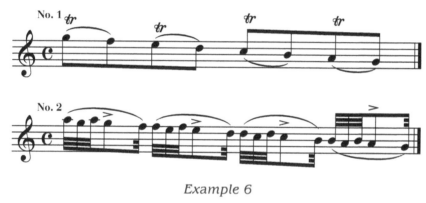

Example 6

If on the contrary the movement is rapid, it is executed as follows *(Example 7)*.

Example 7

The *groupette* which is indicated in this manner (a turn symbol) is also one of those abbreviations which are employed in passages as those of No. 1 of the following example *(Example 8)*, but which must be executed as if written in No. 2 of the same example.

Example 8

There is a great deal more to be said on this subject, but, in my opinion, the view that I have given of it is quite sufficient to show the pupil what is the most essential to be known, the rest will be learned with time and practice.

Thirty Scales

For the Study of the Articulation

A. M.-R. Barret
Edited by Martin Schuring

19

20

22

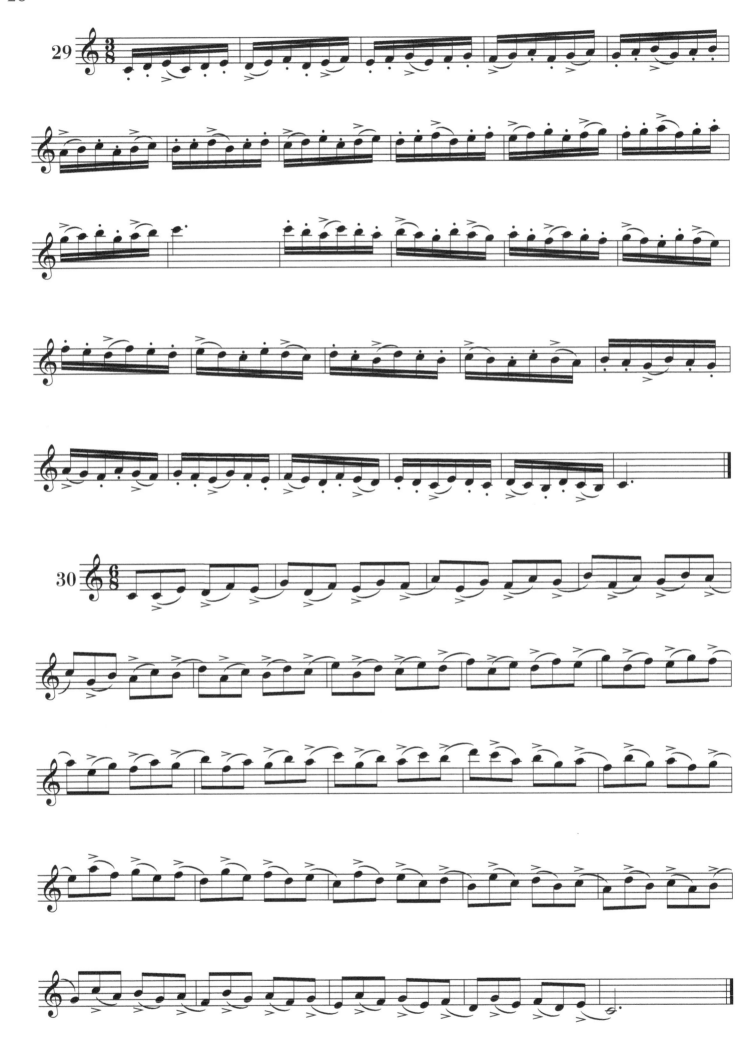

Twelve Articulation Exercises

A. M.-R. Barret
Edited by Martin Schuring

28

Forty Progressive Melodies

A. M.-R. Barret
Edited by Martin Schuring

Allegro moderato. ♩. = 72

54

56

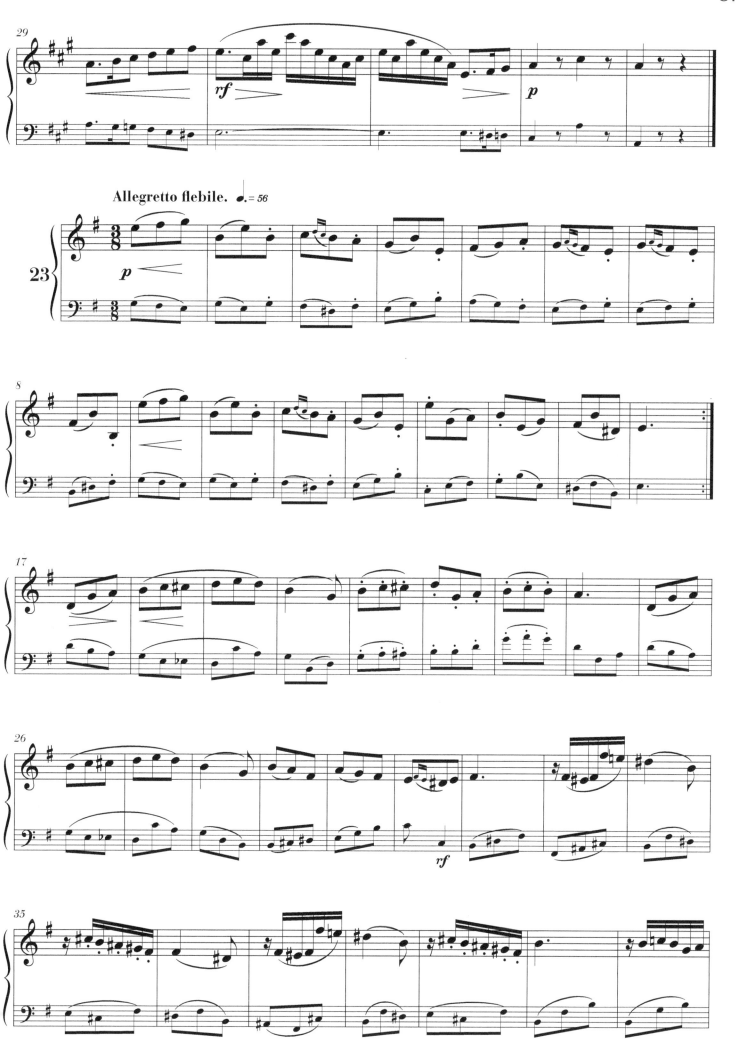

Allegretto flebile. ♩.= 56

Allegro moderato. ♩ = 96

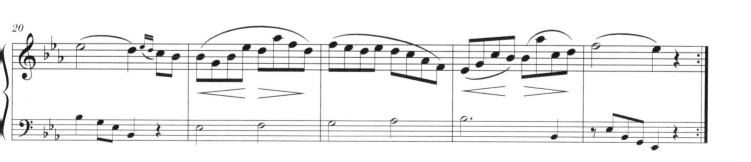

Minuet: Allegro. ♩. = 76

Fine.

Allegro ma non troppo. ♩. = 66

Four Sonatas

Sonata No. 1

A. M.-R. Barret
Edited by Martin Schuring

Sonata No. 2

D.C. al Fine

Sonata No. 3

Sonata No. 4

Andante cantabile. ♪ = 104

D.C. al Fine

Sixteen Grand Studies

A. M.-R. Barret
Edited by Martin Schuring

152

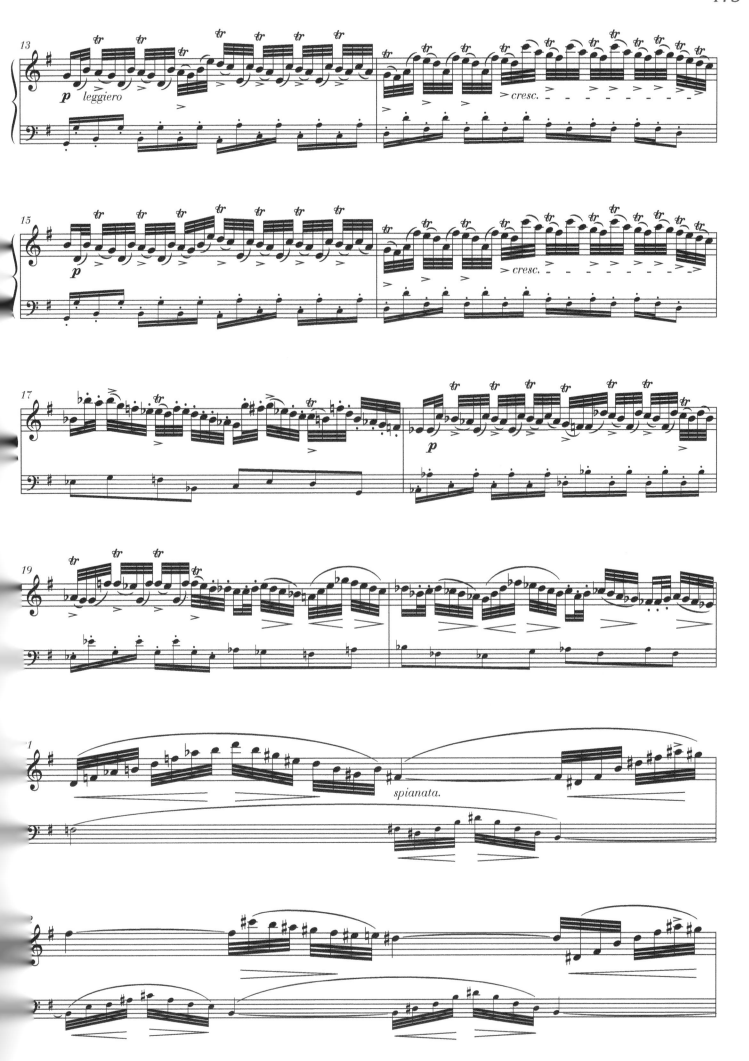

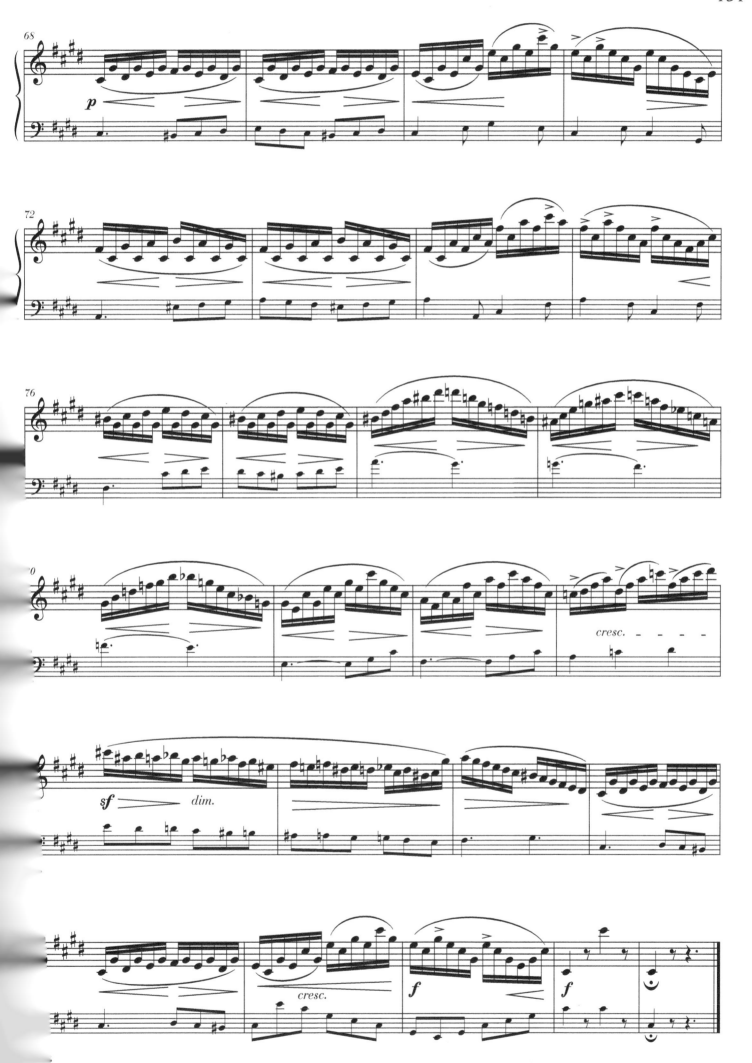